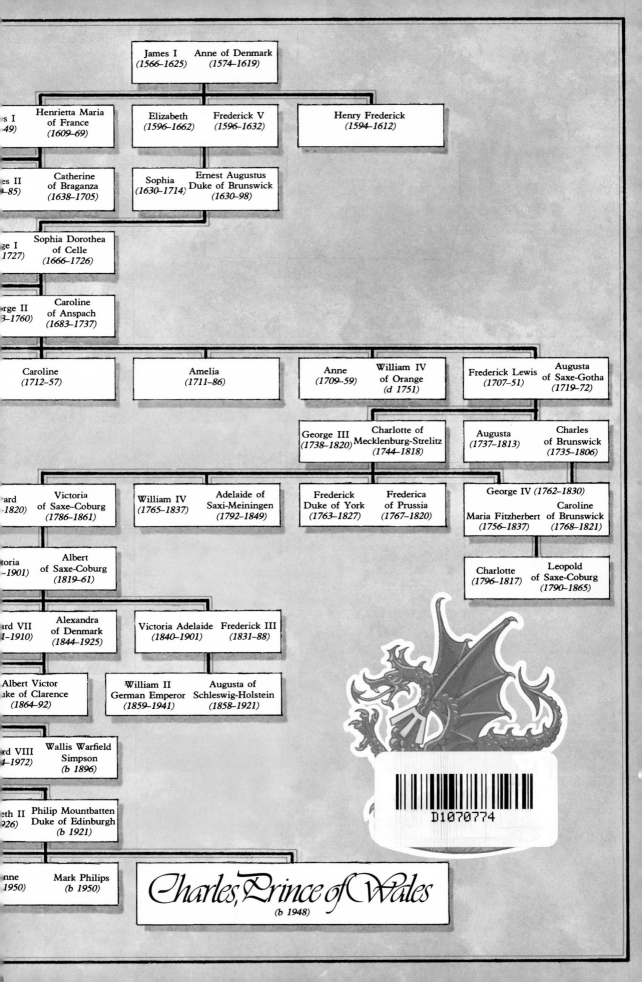

James I
(1566–1625)

Anne of Denmark
(1574–1619)

...s I
...49)

Henrietta Maria
of France
(1609–69)

Elizabeth
(1596–1662)

Frederick V
(1596–1632)

Henry Frederick
(1594–1612)

...es II
...85)

Catherine
of Braganza
(1638–1705)

Sophia
(1630–1714)

Ernest Augustus
Duke of Brunswick
(1630–98)

...e I
...1727)

Sophia Dorothea
of Celle
(1666–1726)

...rge II
...3–1760)

Caroline
of Anspach
(1683–1737)

Caroline
(1712–57)

Amelia
(1711–86)

Anne
(1709–59)

William IV
of Orange
(d 1751)

Frederick Lewis
(1707–51)

Augusta
of Saxe-Gotha
(1719–72)

George III
(1738–1820)

Charlotte of
Mecklenburg-Strelitz
(1744–1818)

Augusta
(1737–1813)

Charles
of Brunswick
(1735–1806)

...ard
...1820)

Victoria
of Saxe–Coburg
(1786–1861)

William IV
(1765–1837)

Adelaide of
Saxi-Meiningen
(1792–1849)

Frederick
Duke of York
(1763–1827)

Frederica
of Prussia
(1767–1820)

George IV (1762–1830)

Maria Fitzherbert
(1756–1837)

Caroline
of Brunswick
(1768–1821)

...toria
...–1901)

Albert
of Saxe-Coburg
(1819–61)

Charlotte
(1796–1817)

Leopold
of Saxe-Coburg
(1790–1865)

...ard VII
...1–1910)

Alexandra
of Denmark
(1844–1925)

Victoria Adelaide
(1840–1901)

Frederick III
(1831–88)

Albert Victor
...uke of Clarence
(1864–92)

William II
German Emperor
(1859–1941)

Augusta of
Schleswig-Holstein
(1858–1921)

...rd VIII
...4–1972)

Wallis Warfield
Simpson
(b 1896)

...eth II
...926)

Philip Mountbatten
Duke of Edinburgh
(b 1921)

...nne
...1950)

Mark Philips
(b 1950)

Charles, Prince of Wales
(b 1948)

Diana
Princess of Wales

Our Future Queen

Brenda Ralph Lewis

Purnell

ISBN 0 361 05433 5

Copyright © 1982 Purnell Publishers Limited
Published 1982 by Purnell Books, Paulton, Bristol BS18 5LQ
Made and printed in Great Britain by Purnell and Sons
(Book Production) Limited, Paulton, Bristol
Colour reproduction by K. L. W. Plates Ltd., London

The months between the announcement of Lady Diana's engagement to Prince Charles and the wedding day itself, were a time of great Press and public interest. Lady Diana became the focal point of worldwide attention and she was unable, it seemed, to leave her own front door without facing a barrage of Press cameramen. Not unnaturally the strain and pressure of such attention caused this rather shy young girl a few anxious moments, as can be seen in these photographs. But even this only endeared her still further to the public, to whom her face was becoming one of the best-known in the world.

ynics would call it a foregone conclusion: no matter who she was, they might say, the girl who married the Prince of Wales and so became Britain's future Queen was bound to become the centre of intense public attention and avid Press and TV coverage. It was, after all, an important royal and dynastic event: when Prince Charles married Lady Diana Spencer at St Paul's Cathedral on 29th July 1981, no heir to the throne had wed as Prince of Wales since 1863, when the later King Edward VII and his Danish bride Alexandra became man and wife.

However if anyone, cynic or no, imagined that Diana, the new Princess of Wales, was riding into the public eye on her husband's personal popularity or on the bandwagon of affection for the Royal Family, they were totally mistaken. From the time of her engagement to Charles on 24th February 1981, and certainly after their wedding five months later, Princess Diana has put her own individual mark on the royal public image. And there is no doubt that she has scored instant and total success.

At the Mansion House luncheon in early November, Charles himself expressed it when he spoke of the "overwhelming effect my dear wife has on everybody". By that time the 'overwhelming effect' had been amply demonstrated by the vast, welcoming crowds who braved downpours of rain and biting winds during Charles and Diana's tour of Wales in late October. It was there again when Diana rode with Princess Anne in the glass coach to attend her first state occasion — the opening of Parliament by the Queen on 4th November. Londoners who packed the pavements to watch the procession go by were charmed by the prettiness of the new Princess and her warm smile, and by how well she had already mastered the famous royal wave. Just over a week later, during the tour of Chesterfield and York, the crowds were openly concerned about Diana, whose expected baby had been announced on 5th November, when they saw her looking pale and clearly none too well.

Both the sympathy and the admiration seem to be a response to the warm-hearted, spontaneous nature Diana not only possesses, but manages to project even when surrounded by thousands of people. Although she is 'blue-blooded' in her own right — an earl's daughter, a member of one of England's most prestigious noble families and the descendant of several kings — she is remarkably unassuming. Diana has no time for sophisticated society life, preferring the countryside and country pursuits, nor

is she especially fond of the jewellery she can well afford to
possess. In fact, Diana is as far from the haughty aristocrat as it is
possible to be. In an age of often strident feminism she's also
delightfully feminine, as well as frankly homeloving and blessed
with a great affection for, and a way with, small children. If, as
she has declared, she wants 'lots and lots' of children, it's because
she loves them, not because it's her duty to provide heirs for the
heir to the throne — the principal and sometimes the only
function of the Royal Consorts of past kings and princes.

Somewhat unusually too, in this permissive age of ours, Diana
has a proper, though not prudish sense of modesty and was none
too pleased at the revealing back-to-the-sunlight pictures taken of
her before her engagement at the Pimlico kindergarten where she
worked: that was the embarrassing day she forgot to wear a
petticoat. Even more upsetting was the rumour that, in October
1980, when the royal romance was just blossoming, Diana met
Charles clandestinely on board the royal train while Charles was
in the West Country. Angry official denials resulted. As it
happens, Diana never set foot on a royal train until a year later, at
the time of the tour of Wales, when Prince Charles introduced
his new Princess to the Welsh people.

Diana has also shown herself touchingly vulnerable on
occasion. She's perfectly capable of blushing in public, and it's
endearing rather than embarrassing. She can get upset and
unnerved — and show it; as she did when confronted with the

Two of the pictures which charmed the world. Lady Diana Spencer, with two of her small charges at the Young England kindergarten in Pimlico, shortly before her engagement to Prince Charles was announced. Leaving the children at the kindergarten was one of Diana's few regrets as she entered the Royal fold. Despite her first crowded weeks as Princess of Wales, she has been back to see them several times.

Her love of children has particularly endeared the Princess to everyone. Small children and toddlers seem to respond to her immediately everywhere she goes.

artillery of Press cameras at Tidworth, while watching Prince Charles playing polo a few days before the wedding. Diana can burst into tears on a sad occasion — as when Charles's favourite horse Allibar suddenly died after an early morning run early in 1981. When Diana is pursued by the more unscrupulous Press into private life — popping down to the shops in Tetbury, or enjoying a short holiday in the Caribbean in February 1982 — public sympathy is solidly behind her. And not just because the Queen was driven on those two occasions to make strong protests.

Palace officials may have had nightmares over the blushes and the tears, or over jokey remarks like the one the Princess made when she switched on Regent Street's Christmas lights in November 1981: "I've left my old man at home, watching the telly!" she quipped. In addition, security men may get jangled nerves when, on her first public tours as Princess of Wales, Diana shook every hand offered to her, and stopped to speak with every tot who caught her eye. However, there's no more endearing way than this of showing a genuine interest in people, and if it makes the Princess tops in popular affection, it's not at all surprising.

It's not surprising, either, that something very much like a love affair has arisen between the Princess and the public, for in a very few months she has completely exploded the expectations of the stuffier officials of the Royal Household. They presumed that it would take years of royal chores, such as unveiling plaques, or reading prepared speeches on formal occasions, to turn a 20-year-old with no experience of royal duties or royal public life into a practised member of what Prince Charles once called the 'family firm'.

In the event, Princess Diana has graduated in her own spontaneous way, and has struck the public as the sort of lively, yet nice, modest young woman every parent would be pleased to have for a daughter.

At the same time, of course, the public was extremely pleased with the prospect of Diana as a future Queen and delighted that Charles should have made a love match with a bride so suitable for the place of Consort she will one day occupy. Despite the label of 'world's most eligible bachelor' attached to Charles when single, constitutional and religious barriers limited his choice a great deal. In addition, over-zealous Press interest not infrequently wrecked his chances by frightening off some of his girl friends of the past. Charles therefore needed, first of all, someone who could survive Press attention and remain discreet about a royal romance: this Diana proved beyond doubt in the hectic weeks before the engagement when she was virtually under journalistic siege.

The girl Prince Charles married also had to have a blameless past with not a breath of scandal attached to her name; she

At a crowded polo match. Charles and Diana were by now officially engaged and it is easy to see that they are both more relaxed in each other's company in public, now that the news has 'broken' to the world.

The affection Princess

Diana has for children, particularly the under-fives, is clearly shown here as she plays quietly with the toddler on her lap. Both she and the child seem happily engrossed with each other and almost oblivious to everything else around them.

needed to be dutiful without being stuffy about it, and prepared, too, to cope with the restraints and also the tedium that is unavoidable in being a modern royal on perpetual show.

All this comprised a very demanding formula, this need for royalty to be traditional, yet modern at the same time. When, at last, Charles found in Lady Diana Spencer the girl who was the answer to that formula, the problems it posed the Prince — who always said his wife would have to be 'a pretty unusual person' — had helped to delay his marriage till he was at least seven years older than average. Charles's cousins, the Dukes of Kent and Gloucester, both of them likewise married to commoners, wed in their mid-twenties, as did his father, Prince Philip. Charles was 32 and at their engagement, joked that Diana "will keep me young". Nevertheless, if Charles had to wait a while, no one is complaining now, for no one doubts that Princess Diana was worth waiting for. In fact, she made the most popular and most gladly welcomed royal bride anyone can remember.

She also brings with her an extra bonus, for her unvarnished good looks make her particularly suitable for another facet of her public role as a royal. As a public figure under constant scrutiny, the Princess of Wales has to tread a fine line between appearing neither too dowdy, nor too 'way out'. Royals have always been fashion pace setters, but these days, as with royal behaviour and

demeanour, it's expected they won't stray too far from th traditional. The Princess of Wales certainly scores on th account. She's a very pretty girl, but not the glamorous sor whose good looks can be alienating. Her hairstyle, much copie at the time of her engagement and since, is casual yet we groomed, and suitable for tiaras, hats, or no headgear at all. Th style also stresses Diana's friendly informality, a characteristi always appreciated in modern royalty.

Fortunately, for someone who must face popping camera wherever she goes, the Princess is photogenic. It's not ever young woman, either, who has her image on postage stamps – for the wedding and also her 21st birthday on 1st July 1982 – and on medallions, crockery and the multitude of other souvenir that went on sale at the time of the wedding. So, Diana's empath with the camera is doubly fortuitous.

Her youth, too, is an advantage when it comes to fashion. O the threshold of her twenties, no one expects Diana to wear stai 'middle aged' clothes simply because she's the second lady in th land. Instead, she's been able to strike out along her ow distinctive lines, with her favourite frills, lacy collars, low-heele shoes to cope with her above-average height, pearl chokers and wide variety of colours. She has been seen in the filmy pastels sh wore on her honeymoon in the Mediterranean, the red plai

In recent years the Royal 'walkabout' has become something of a tradition as well as a pleasure for members of the Royal Family and the public. It provides an ideal opportunity for Royalty and people to meet and chat in an informal and friendly way. It's not surprising, then, that Diana quickly adopted the walkabout style and, in her relaxed and warm manner, let people get to know their future queen.

On 22 May 1981 Diana and Prince Charles visited Tetbury General Hospital and while in the area took the opportunity to say hello to their future neighbours in the small Cotswold village. This must have been a particularly pleasurable time for everyone. The Royal couple's new home, Highgrove House, is only a short distance away and the people of Tetbury turned out in force to greet them as Lady Diana got her first taste of a typical walkabout welcome. Seeing the smile on her face and the flowers in her hand, it certainly looks as if she enjoyed it just as much as the crowd did.

Above, Lady Diana enjoys a quiet moment alone in her car, away from all the fuss and attention of Press and public. Right, attending a film première in aid of the disabled. Looking quite resplendent in a red and gold-spangled strappy evening gown, with matching gold purse, the future princess once again illustrated her enviable and most useful ability to look marvellous, whatever the occasion.

Below, Lady Diana gives a sweet and secretive smile as she enters her car after the final fitting for the wedding dress
that was to prove a talking point for weeks afterwards. Below right, Lady Diana, Queen Elizabeth the Queen Mother and Princess Margaret chat to Prince Charles before his ill-fated ride on Good Prospect at Sandown Park in March 1981. Unfortunately, Good Prospect did not complete the course and threw the Prince at the eighteenth fence. Lady Diana's suit, with matching hat, looks dashing without being too informal.
Far right, here we see Lady Diana in a more casual sunny mood.

outfit with matching tam o'shanter at the Braemar Games in September, the mauve, beige, midnight blue and emerald she wore in Wales, the postbox-red hat and coat which made such a pleasant splash of colour when she and Prince Charles went to Guildford Cathedral in December, and the peacock blue she wore when she went to church with the rest of the Royal Family on Christmas Day, 1981.

The Princess manages a rare trick — looking good in all these hues — and also setting a new royal style with her off-the-shoulder evening dresses. It was, of course, the stunning black taffeta gown designed by David and Elizabeth Emmanuel which she wore on 9th March 1981 at her first public appearance as Charles's fiancée, which gave notice that a whole new style in royal fashions had arrived. Consequently, the wedding dress by the same designers became an avid talking point long before the wedding day, and on the day itself excited as much interest as the bride who wore it.

Both the black taffeta dress and the wedding gown were copied and in the dress shops within two days and only five hours, respectively. The Diana style has, in fact, proved a tremendous boon to the fashion business at a time of deep recession: as was revealed in February 1982, the demand for her style in frilly blouses, hats and dresses saved thousands of jobs which would otherwise have sunk into redundancy. Likewise, Britain's photographic agencies have virtually had to set up Diana departments to deal with the world-wide demand for pictures of her. One large British agency has found that Diana pictures comprise forty percent of their orders. Her photograph has even appeared on toothpaste advertisements in faraway Brazil.

No one, in the Royal Family or out of it, has made such a leap in so short a time from quiet private life — caring for the children in the Pimlico kindergarten, going down London's Kings Road for a sweater or a pair of jeans — into so great a blaze of public notice that the whole world knows who she is and what she looks like. It's not often, either, that anyone has been taken so quickly to the nation's heart with so complete a lack of reservation. However, the enormous interest in Princess Diana is by no means just a piece of curious celebrity-watching, for the British public has quickly discovered the truth which Diana's father, Earl Spencer, expressed on the day the royal engagement was announced. "A very nice person to have in your family," he said.

The Royal Family or otherwise.

Lord Mountbatten of Burma had always been a firm favourite with Prince Charles and indeed with everyone in the Royal Family, who referred to him as 'Uncle Dickie'. His illustrious career was brought to a sudden and tragic end when he was killed in a bomb explosion on board his boat in 1979. In July of 1981 Lady Diana, accompanied by Prince Charles, ceremonially planted a tree in the grounds of Broadlands, the home of Lord Mountbatten. The couple later spent the first part of their honeymoon at Broadlands, before embarking on their Mediterranean cruise.

On the same day Prince Charles and Lady Diana snatched a brief moment to share a private word. Once again Lady Diana is wearing one of the pretty ruffled outfits she is so fond of, and which have exerted such influence in the world of fashion.
Right, the Princess looks particularly attractive in this casual country outfit, as she pauses while out for a stroll with Prince Charles and his pet labrador Harvey. Both the Prince and Princess of Wales love the countryside and a country way of life.

These pictures of Lady Diana were taken at Tidworth on 25 July 1981, where once again she was watching her future husband playing his favourite sport of polo. This was the day that Diana was a little upset by the rather over-zealous attentions of the Press photographers, pressure she has since learned to cope with as all the Royals must do. But there are no signs of tears in these three photographs, where Lady Diana is wearing a delightfully pretty floral-printed skirt and waistcoast in blues and greens, along with matching mauve shoes and clutch bag. She sits with Lord Romsey, behind and to her left, with whom she shares a joke.

Below, before Princes Charles begins his match the Royal couple are the centre of attention for everyone!

The Royal Family have always been closely connected with, and taken a strong interest in, the armed forces and it's no surprise, therefore, that one of the Prince and Lady Diana's official engagements should be with the Army!

On the Saturday before their wedding, Prince Charles and Lady Diana paid a visit to Chelsea Barracks, where they met the soldiers and their families. The children crowded to the window to wave Diana goodbye as she left (far right).

Right, a lad of four months, who must be her youngest admirer, gave the soon-to-be Princess of Wales a rosebud. Left, even a future Queen has to contend with unruly hair when it's a blustery day! Below, as crowds look on, Prince Charles and Lady Diana leave the barracks, carrying a well-earned bouquet of flowers and accompanied by what looks like a very friendly military escort. By the happy looks on everyone's faces, they all seem to have had an enjoyable day!

...e wedding that enthralled ...world.

...left, wearing her gorgeous ...feta wedding dress, Lady ...na enters St Paul's ...thedral on the arm of her ...her, Earl Spencer. Ahead of ...m both is the long walk up ...aisle of the cathedral to ...ere Prince Charles waits.

...t and top, the Princess of ...les emerges from St Paul's ...the arm of her husband, ...rying a luxuriant bouquet ...flowers. Prince Charles ...ars the uniform of Royal

Navy Commander.
Right, the Royal couple begin their ride home from the cathedral. Now the cheering crowds have an opportunity to see that famous wedding dress and the Spencer family diamond tiara worn by the new Princess of Wales.

Crowds lined the entire processional route from St Paul's to Buckingham Palace. A group of Brownies (above) wait to tell Princes Charles and Princess Diana what they probably already know!

Lady Diana Spencer joins her future in-laws at a right Royal occasion: the Ascot races, in June 1981. The successive days at Ascot unmistakably demonstrated Diana's fashion style: plenty of frills, bows, candy-stripes and cute hats. Above, a lightweight mauve suit, perfectly in keeping with the summery atmosphere of Ascot. Above right, with Prince Charles in top hat and tails. Right, there's a hint of the nautical about this outfit.

Above, Lady Diana wearing a lovely peach-coloured dress with ruff and matching boater.

Below and right, with Prince Charles on the Opening Day of Royal Ascot.

The Prince and Princess's wedding presents, including those from children, were exhibited at St James's Palace. The exhibition raised £86,000 for the Royal Wedding Souvenir Fund for the Disabled by the time it closed on 4 October. Below, Prince Charles and Princess Diana on the deck of the Royal yacht Britannia, as the ship prepares to cast off.

Right, Prince Charles and his new Princess flew in to Gibraltar to start a quiet, strictly secluded honeymoon cruise in the Mediterranean.
Below, Britannia left Gibraltar with a mass of small ships giving the Royal couple a joyful and noisy send-off.
Far right, all good cruises come to an end. The Prince and Princess at Hurghada, the Egyptian military airfield where the late President Sadat and his wife Jihan came to see them off as they boarded an RAF VC-10 to return home.

The two-week cruise in the Mediterranean was followed by another eleven honeymooning at Balmoral, which Diana considers one of the most beautiful places in the world. By tacit agreement, the Royal Family is left strictly alone during their holidays at Balmoral each summer. The Prince and Princess did, however, agree to meet the Press and TV at a quiet spot by the River Dee, she in warm country tweeds, he in kilt and pullover. When asked how she was enjoying married life, the Princess replied: "I can recommend it!" The subsequent pictures taken of the happy Royal couple more than confirmed that comment.

Princess Diana's first big
royal engagement was a
thorough-going triumph.
Everywhere the Royal couple
appeared during their three-
day tour of the Principality of
Wales, there were smiling,
cheering crowds, a sea of
waving Union Jacks and the
Princess's ladies-in-waiting
swamped by the flowers that
were given to her. If anything,
the Princess entered into the
happy spirit of the event a bit
too enthusiastically. She shook
so many hands that her own
soon become red and sore. She
also put the Royal timetable
in danger by stopping so
frequently to talk with people
in the crowd. Above, the Royal
couple attended a gala in
Swansea during their trip.

Above left, the tour of Wales started on a decidedly windy day at Rhyl. The Princess wore a charming red and black outfit, though she did have trouble keeping her hat on! Above right, more people to meet and more hands to shake! Once again the people of Wales express their love for their new Princess by giving her beautiful bouquets of flowers. Above, one of the Princess's most delightful costumes. A rich plum-coloured jacket, and hat of velvet are set off with a white ruff and a simple pearl choker, another of the Princess's favourites. The picture illustrates the ease with which the Princess's hair-style can be adapted to suit a more formal occasion. Right, from Rhyl the Royal couple's tour of Wales took them to Llandudno and Caernarvon. Far right, in Cardiff the Prince and Princess of Wales received the freedom of the City. The Princess wore a gorgeous blue and gold dress, complemented by sapphire and diamond earrings. It was here that she made her first speech in Welsh.

ICH DIEN

Far left, Prince Charles's marriage meant sharing a coat of arms with his wife. The Prince's arms showing the lions of England are on the left, the Princess's Spencer family arms on the right.

Left, Christmas Day, 1981. Princess Diana, wearing an embroidered peacock-blue coat and hat, with the rest of the Royal Family, after attending the Christmas Day service at St George's Chapel, Windsor.

Below and far left, planting a tree near the Royal Thames Yacht Club premises in London's Hyde Park, in November 1981.

Centre, switching on Regent Street's Christmas lights was the first public engagement the Princess of Wales fulfilled without her husband.

Below left, at the Dick Sheppard School in Brixton, late in 1981.

Above and below, riding next to Princess Anne in the same glass coach which carried her to her wedding, the Princess of Wales goes to her first full-dress state occasion: the Opening of Parliament by the Queen on 4 November. Right, a newcomer at the traditional royal engagement: Lady Diana Spencer stands next to the splendidly uniformed Prince Charles, watching the Trooping of the

*olour ceremony from the
alcony of Buckingham
alace. Just over five weeks
ter, Charles and Diana were
ce more out on the balcony,
acknowledge the cheers of
e crowd on their wedding
ay.*

bove and right, in early

*September, while still on
honeymoon, the Princess of
Wales attended the Highland
Games at Braemar with other
members of the Royal Family.
There is a distinctly Scottish
look to this charming costume
of plaid dress and beret,
entirely fitting to the day.*

Above and far left, a delighted Prince Charles leaves
the Lindo Wing of St Mary's Hospital, Paddington,
after the birth of his son.
Centre, the official notice of the Royal birth, which
appeared outside Buckingham Palace.
Left and below, the Prince and Princess of Wales left
St Mary's on 22 June with their son who was born at
three minutes past nine on the evening of 21 June. The
baby weighed 7 lb 1½ oz.

Above, the Princess of Wales is greeted on her arrival at Gloucester Cathedral. At York in November (above left) the Princess spent ninety minutes touring the National Railway Museum, and at Chesterfield (left) opened a new shopping precinct and a police headquarters. Above far right, Princess Diana drove herself down in December from Highgrove House to fulfil a promise to visit St Mary's Junior School in Tetbury. Above right, right and far right, the Prince and Princess opened the new Barbican Arts Centre in March 1982.

*…the opening of The
…lendours of the Gonzaga
…hibition at the Victoria and
…bert Museum, London, in
…e autumn of 1981. The
…rincess of Wales looked
…mply stunning and very regal
…deed in her beautiful blue,
…auve, pink and white off-the-
…oulder gown. Again she wore
…e of her favourite pearl
…okers, this time with
…atching diamond tear-drop
…rrings. This surely must be
…e of the most beautiful
…esses she has worn,
…immering as it did in soft
…le shades. Everywhere she
…es the Princess impresses
…th her warmth and radiant
…mininity and her day at the
…ictoria and Albert Museum
…s a perfect example of this.*

The Princess of Wales

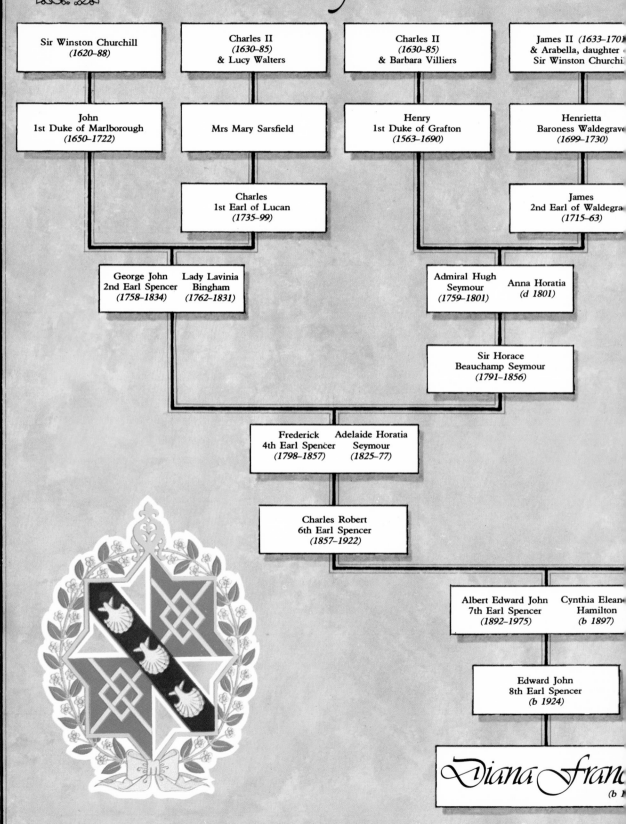

Sir Winston Churchill
(1620–88)

Charles II
(1630–85)
& Lucy Walters

Charles II
(1630–85)
& Barbara Villiers

James II *(1633–1701)*
& Arabella, daughter
Sir Winston Churchill

John
1st Duke of Marlborough
(1650–1722)

Mrs Mary Sarsfield

Henry
1st Duke of Grafton
(1563–1690)

Henrietta
Baroness Waldegrave
(1699–1730)

Charles
1st Earl of Lucan
(1735–99)

James
2nd Earl of Waldegrave
(1715–63)

George John
2nd Earl Spencer
(1758–1834)

Lady Lavinia
Bingham
(1762–1831)

Admiral Hugh
Seymour
(1759–1801)

Anna Horatia
(d 1801)

Sir Horace
Beauchamp Seymour
(1791–1856)

Frederick
4th Earl Spencer
(1798–1857)

Adelaide Horatia
Seymour
(1825–77)

Charles Robert
6th Earl Spencer
(1857–1922)

Albert Edward John
7th Earl Spencer
(1892–1975)

Cynthia Eleanor
Hamilton
(b 1897)

Edward John
8th Earl Spencer
(b 1924)

Diana Frances
(b 1...)